BLACK-ON-BLACK CRIME IN AMERICA

Dr. Daniel Williams, Jr.

BK Royston Publishing
P. O. Box 4321
Jeffersonville, IN 47131
502-802-5385
http://www.bkroystonpublishing.com
bkroystonpublishing@gmail.com

© Copyright – 2022

All Rights Reserved. No part of this book may be reproduced, stored in a retrieval system, or transmitted by any means without the written permission of the author.

Cover Design: Elite Book Covers

ISBN-13: 978-1-959543-12-1

Printed in the United States of America

Dedication

To my beloved mother, Corine Powe Williams, I dedicate this book to you. You are the one who trained, encouraged, and inspired me to become the man I have become. I am honored to have a great mother like you and be your son.
I thank God for you, mom.

Acknowledgements

Inspired by the Word of God, I felt compelled to write this book.

Without the grace of God, this book would not have come to fruition. I am so thankful and honored that God has chosen me to be the author of this book. This book is a gift from Him to the American people and the human race.

As Americans, we have a lot to be grateful and thankful for. America is the greatest country in this world!

If I had the money, I would offer every American the opportunity to visit an underdeveloped country or a third-world country so that he or she could see how other people are living in this world.

Jesus Christ, my Lord, and Redeemer is the Way, Truth, and Life. He has laid down His Life so that we can have eternal life.

Thank you, my Lord and Savior!!

Something To Think About

Every black man is not your brother, and every white man is not your enemy.
~Dr. Daniel Williams Jr.

A person who knows everything cannot learn anything because he or she knows everything. When a person stops learning, he or she becomes like a withered flower; he or she dies!
~Dr. Daniel Williams Jr.

There is a thin line between love and hate, but it is better to love, not to hate.
~Dr. Daniel Williams Jr.

Love is contagious when people know that they are loved.
~Dr. Daniel Williams Jr.

If a person cannot give life, she or he does not have a right to take someone's else life.
~Dr. Daniel Williams Jr.

The majority of America will become the minority; and the minority will become the majority.
~Dr. Daniel Williams Jr.

Healthy black men rear healthy black families.
~Dr. Daniel Williams Jr.

A man who does not know his past has no future.
~Dr. Daniel Williams Jr.

Writing a book is like putting together a jigsaw puzzle.
~Dr. Daniel Williams Jr.

Women use sex to get love, and men use love to get sex.
~Dr. Daniel Williams Jr.

Life is about relationships.
~Dr. Daniel Williams Jr.

Table Of Contents

Dedication	iii
Acknowledgements	v
Something to Think About	vii
Introduction	xiii
Preface	xv
Chapter 1 **What Is Black-On-Black Crime?**	1
Chapter 2 **Black People Need To Pull Themselves By Their Bootstraps**	15
Chapter 3 **Ideology of Black-On-Black Crime**	21
Chapter 4 **Dynamics of Black-On-Black Crime**	27
Chapter 5 **A Perspective of Black History**	31
Chapter 6 **Is Black-On-Black Crime a Social Disease or a Maladaptive Behavior?**	39
Chapter 7 **Black Hip-hop/Rap Music: As It Relates to Black-On-Black Crime**	45
Chapter 8 **No Snitching**	51

Chapter 9 Redlining: As It Relates to Black-On-Black Crime	57
Chapter 10 Black-On-Black Crime vs. White-On-White Crime	63
Chapter 11 Gentrification: As It Relates to Black-On-Black Crime	71
Chapter 12 A Comparative Analysis of Domestic Violence Between Black Families and White Families	77
Chapter 13 The White Flight: As It Relates to Black-On-Black Crime	81
Chapter 14 Carjacking	85
Chapter 15 A Perspective of People of Color	89
Chapter 16 The Majority Becomes the Minority and the Minority Becomes the Majority	95
Chapter 17 A Perspective of Black Mortality	99

Chapter 18   **103**
The American Dream: As It Relates to Black-On-Black Crime

Chapter 19   **109**
L.I.T.S. (Leadership Integrating Tomorrow's Souls)

Purchase at: www.amazon.com

Introduction

Black-on-black crime is dear to me, because I have been a victim of this crime numerous times when I was living in the *hood* during my childhood and early adolescent years. Moreover, I am a black man, and I want to make a difference in America by addressing this chronic problem.

In my previous book (**Why Do Americans Hate Americans?**), I stated that **black-on-black crime** is just as serious as racism in America. The majority of the non-African Americans I interviewed believe that **black-on-black crime** is a problem that only blacks can resolve themselves. Interestingly, some African Americans feel the same. I disagree. If this were the case, I would not be writing about this chronic social disease that has been infesting our society for decades. I do not believe these individuals know the scope or magnitude of **black-on-black crime** in America. Some African Americans believe that it is a hopeless situation, claiming there are too many barriers involved in this societal issue. Looking at this phenomenon from a different perspective, I believe the situation is not hopeless. At the end of this book, I will provide some suggestions, methods, ideas to combat **black-on-black crime** in America. However, since I am a pragmatic, visionary person, I will be approaching this issue in a sensible and realistic way. It is my hope that the mainstream will provide support and resources, to help eradicate **black-on-black crime** in our great country!

Preface

Black-on-black crime continues to be an avoided *epidemic* in America. Similarly, it is treated as racism, i.e., people know it is a problem but refuse to address it. The main underlying problem of **black-on-black crime** is the lack of economic opportunities in the black communities. For instance, poverty, redlining, gentrification, as well as racism, are evident in black communities where **black-on-black crime** is rampant. Cities such as Chicago, Compton, Baltimore, L.A., Detroit, Philadelphia and Austin, Texas, have some of the highest homicide rates in America due to blacks killing blacks. Gun control is not the answer. I have often heard that guns do not kill people; people kill people. There may be some validity to this. However, the argument is how do guns get into the black communities? This is the same argument I hear people say about drugs in the black communities. Well, I believe it is not that simple. And it is not that black and white. Variables such as unemployment, high school dropout, teenage pregnancy and absent fathers play a significant role in **black-on-black crime** in our country.

It is my belief that **black-on-black crime** can be eradicated, provided there are economic opportunities and <u>quality education</u> provided to <u>all</u> African Americans, especially those who live in the inner cities and urban areas in America.

My purpose of writing this book is to help people to become aware of this social disease and help eradicate **black-on-black crime** in America. Moreover, non-African Americans who are not versed in **black-on-black crime** will be better informed about this topic, after reading this book. At least, that's my aim!

Chapter 1
What Is Black-On Black Crime?

I had been under the false assumption that everyone knows about **black-on-black crime** in America, until I started talking to non-African Americans about this social disease in our country. I have been enlightened and educated by non-African Americans about their perspectives and perceptions of **black-on-black crime** in America. Surprisingly, some of the white people to whom I have spoken have never heard of this concept. In fact, many of these individuals had very little or no contact with blacks when they were in grade school. These individuals lived in communities where blacks did not live or were not seen. Admittedly, I was extraordinarily astounded hearing this. Naively, I assumed that all Americans had contact with blacks. Obviously, I was <u>grossly</u> mistaken.

Black-on-black crime is a phenomenon that has been in existence since the creation of man. It is a social disease that does not seem to have any limits or any ending of its existence. **Black-on-black crime** is physical assault that black people inflict on each other, as well as stealing from each other. For instance, black street gangs are notorious for killing each other as well as innocent bystanders, including babies and children who are black. Black street gangs have been known to kill their rival's family members, including small children, who have nothing to do with their fathers' involvement in gangs. One of the people I interviewed about this reported that she saw a news coverage reporting that a rival gang member kidnapped his rival father's child and killed the child in an alley. Unbelievable!!

During my childhood and early adolescent years, my family and I lived in the *hood* where there was rampant **black-on-black crime**. Constant sounds of gunshots and sirens throughout the day and night were the norm. People were killed and their bodies were dumped in alleys on a daily basis. When I would travel from one black neighborhood to another black neighborhood, I was very cognizant of the different gangs, wanting to avoid trouble and not become a victim of **black-on-black crime**.

Schools used to be a haven for children in America. We did not have so much violence in schools as we see today. Children would be able to attend school without being concerned about being injured and/or killed. Now, schools, especially black schools, across our nation are rampant with school violence and/or school shootings.

I can recall the very first time I personally experienced and witnessed school violence. I was in the eighth grade, returning from lunch and waiting to be allowed inside the school building. (The grade school I attended at the time was located in the "Disciple territory," but predominantly "Black Stone Rangers" attended the school). This school was totally hell! Every day I would have to fight gang members from both sides, in order to attend school and leave to go home from school.

This one particular day was quite unusual: While I and other students were waiting to be allowed in the school building, returning from lunch, some of the students were shouting out gang slogans when they recognized their rival gang was walking by, not driving by. The rival gang members opened fire on us. I heard bullets ricocheting off the school building, inches over my head. The Chicago police officer who was assigned to provide safety and security to my school (James Wadsworth Elementary), returned gunfire. I could not believe what my ears were hearing. I was just a few feet from the officer as he exchanged gunfire with the

Disciple gang members. This was not the only time that someone shot at me. In my junior year in high school (Fenger Academy High School), I was leaving to go home after a fight broke out at a house party. As I was walking toward 103rd and Michigan, I heard the same familiar sounds of bullets ricocheting off the building. Immediately, I ran for cover, looking back to make sure I was not being followed or chased. What was so intriguing about this incident was that I came face-to-face with the shooter months later. Interestingly, he admitted shooting at me, but he thought I was someone else. He apologized and asked if I was hit by his gunshots, and I said, "No." This conversation took place on a CTA bus on 111th and Wallace, while my buddy and I were going home from basketball practice. Mysteriously, I felt somewhat embarrassed, because other people on the bus, including my buddy, were listening to the conversation. So, I quickly ended the conversation, stating that I was OK. My buddy never asked about the details of the conversation with this gang member. As the gang member was exiting the bus, he nodded at me, as if he seemed to be concerned. (Ironically, the same gang member who shot at me in my junior year of high school is the same gang member who tried to recruit me when I was a freshman in high school.) House parties were very popular, when I was in high school. I tried to attend them as often as I could. But I stopped attending them after the shooting incident. Instead, I decided to attend parties in downtown Chicago. They were usually sponsored by adults and safer to attend. Of course, I would have to pay to get in these parties.

The majority of the inner cities in America have a serious problem with **black-on-black crime**, particularly major cities such as Chicago, L.A., Compton, Detroit, Philadelphia, Washington D.C., Baltimore, the Bronx, just to name a few.

The majority of **black-on-black crime** is committed by black street gangs, involving street drugs, turf dispute and disrespect. Many Americans, including African Americans, wonder why there is so much self-hatred and senseless killing among blacks. **Why do blacks hate blacks?** This would be a fair question to ask. People I interviewed believe that many of the black youth don't or never had positive male role models in their lives; and some believe many of these youth are lost and have some psychological issues. They never developed a conscience, i.e., learning to do what is right and knowing the difference between right and wrong. Psychologically, there may be some truth to this, based on the research I have reviewed. Research shows that black youth involved in street gangs have been diagnosed with Conduct Disorder, Oppositional Defiant Disorder or Antisocial Personality Disorder. My experience working with gang members provided me with some interesting intricates and insights about strect gangs in general.

Gang members consider their gangs as their family. Many of the gang members believe their time on earth is limited. In fact, the majority of them do not believe they will live beyond 18. In fact, the Department of Justice (DOJ) verifies this.

One of the gang members I worked with had an interesting story. At the time I was working with him, he had been shot three times and was treated for depression. When I questioned him about his affiliation with the gang, he stated that he had no interest in getting out of the gang, because he was taking care of his family. Besides, his mother knew about his gang involvement. This kid was only 15 years old. What's so interesting about this gang member's story is that it is not unusual. Even though gang members realize their lives are short, they believe that it is a way to make a living. The majority of gang members are high school dropouts, or never attended high school. They have no job experience or trade other than drug trafficking and/or gang banging. Unfortunately, this contributes to the death morality rate for African Americans, which is one of the factors that causes the lack of growth among African Americans. The population rate of African Americans is between 12% and 13%, and this rate has been pretty much constant since WWII.

According to the DOJ, African Americans commit more crimes than non-African Americans. **Black-on-black crime** tends to be more severe and deadly for blacks compared to non-African Americans. An African American is more likely to become a fatal gun-shot victim than a non-African American regardless of his or her socioeconomic status (SES). In other words, it does not matter where African Americans live or their SES, they, too, are at a higher risk of **black-on-black crime**.

During the writing of this book, something extraordinarily happened between two black celebrity men in the view of the world: It was the slap that Will Smith planted on Chris Rock's face during the Oscars in March 2022. Without getting into the details that led to the incident, it demonstrates the epitome of **black-on-black crime**. This is exactly how the world perceives blacks, particularly black men, as violent and vicious. There is no excuse for violence. Two black men, who are well known to the American public, are the main attraction in the media. An attraction that is not uncommon to white Americans.

Too often there is criticism and outcry when blacks are attacked, injured, or killed by white people or White Supremacist groups or the KKK, but very little self-examination of **black-on-black crime** is explored. Regardless of who commits assault, it is a crime. Crime should be addressed accordingly. Period.

Typically, when white people see blacks fighting and killing themselves, they sit back watch and point their fingers. "See there, let them kill themselves." And we wonder why when blacks are terrorized and killed, nothing comes of it. In essence, there are no consequences of hurting or killing a black man, because the world perceives him as worthless, useless and insignificant! The Will Smith and Chris Rock incident is a perfect example of this. Hence, Will Smith is not held accountable for his repulsive and violent behavior.

Chapter 2

Black People Need to Pull Themselves by Their Bootstraps

It amazes me to hear so many Americans, including African Americans, saying that black people need to pull themselves by their bootstraps, meaning blacks need to help themselves. Obviously, there is no sympathy from these individuals. In response, I tell them it's not that easy. If it were, I would not be writing about this chronic social issue in our great country. I am often asked what I did to make my life better and not become like the other unfortunate blacks. My response is always "by the ***grace of God!***" There is no way I could have made it out of that *hellhole* by my own merits. When I tell people this, they don't believe me. Oh well!

I don't care who you are or where you came from, no one comes into this world and becomes successful without help! I know this first-hand. Some people may want to believe they did not have anyone to help them as they took their journey in life. We all have been helped, even if you don't acknowledge or believe it. God did not put people in a vacuum so that they can live life independently. Life does not work that way. Unfortunately, there are people who claimed that no one helped them in life. Personally, I don't believe it!

In 1917, the Greenwood District of Tulsa, Oklahoma, was developed, making it one of the prosperous communities in the United States of America. In fact, it became known as the *Black Wall Street*. This black community was self-sufficient, independent, efficient, productive, and rich!! It had its own bank, hotel, hospital, theater, schools, shops, grocery stores, and many professional businesses. Moreover, it was a flourishing community! What was so amazing about this community is that all the money stayed within its own community, making it independent from the American mainstream economy. It had its own economy and infrastructure. Blacks, indeed, pulled themselves by their bootstraps. Unfortunately, the success of the *Black Wall Street* was short lived.

In 1921, Tulsa's Greenwood District was completely destroyed by white people due to jealousy and lies. It was a massacre: mobs of white people attacked the community. Bombs were dropped from airplanes, killing hundreds of innocents — successful blacks — and destroying black businesses. Black women, children and men were lynched. When all the smoke cleared, the community was demolished!! Interestingly, a similar situation occurred in Rosewood, Florida, the next year, but not to the extent that the Greenwood District encountered. But Rosewood, Florida, was also a black community. However, it was not as successful as the *Black Wall Street*, but it was able to hold its own, economically! What's my point?

If *Black Wall Street* once existed in America, people cannot accuse black people of not doing anything to help themselves. Black people do have the capability, knowledge, skills, and ingenuity to be successful, productive and industrious in America. The issue is what impact would *black success* have on America, especially on blacks? Would there be another *Black Wall Street* massacre? Would blacks be safe if they were to have another *Black Wall Street*? That remains to be seen.

Reflection

Chapter 3

Ideology of Black-On-Black Crime

The ideology of **black-on-black crime** may be mysterious and a myth. The way black people think, conceptualize, internalize or rationalize **black-on-black crime** is intriguing and elusive. Nevertheless, we know that *White Supremacy*, *White Superiority and Whiteness* are implicated. These three concepts perpetuate racist views, stereotypes, racism and oppression of black people, underscoring **black-on-black crime** in America. As a result of this, many blacks, if not the majority, have internalized these destructive views of themselves.

Even though there is a lot of blame placed on blacks for their plight, we know that *White Supremacy*, *White Superiority* and *Whiteness* weigh heavily on the minds of Americans, especially black people. Black people know the negative history of *White Supremacy, White Superiority and Whiteness*, causing blacks to think, behave and live as they are portrayed and perceived by the mainstream of our society, especially the media. Unfortunately, **black-on-black crime** is a result of this.

Within the black race, blacks tend to reinforce the stereotypes, perceptions, bias and racist views about themselves. For instance, blacks are portrayed as intellectually inferior and dangerous. These are some of the same stereotypes blacks have about each other. It is believed that blacks do not value life; they are perceived to be aimless and unproductive. Blacks complain that other blacks behave in the same manner they are seen in subordinate roles in movies, involving characters who do not have any substance to their roles, as well as in public.

Perpetrators of **black-on-black crime** have taken on the racist worldviews and biases that devalue their self-worth, dignity, self-respect and a lack of love for their own black communities. Consequently, this creates a division and a system of oppression in the black communities.

According to the dictionary, oppression is defined as "unjust or cruel exercise of authority or power." For instance, when blacks are unjustly oppressed by an authority figure or "the power that be," this is a form of oppression. Oppression is one of the tenets of racism. Without oppression, there is no racism. Hence, oppression is implicated in **black-on-black crime** in America.

Race plays an integral part in racism, too. Generally, blacks are oppressed by certain organizations, authorities, groups, economically, because of their race. Now, there are two ways racism is exhibited — covertly and overtly. Covert racism is subtle and not necessarily obvious, whereas overt racism is obvious and pretty much "in your face."

Black people, who do not live in predominantly black communities, tend to separate themselves from the impoverished black communities where **black-on-black crime** is a norm, as well as a lifestyle for black perpetrators. Interestingly, these same individuals try to identify with the oppressor by internalizing their problematic worldviews, beliefs and values, while belittling other blacks, without knowing it.

Having a low self-esteem, disrespect for one's race and/or oneself and having feelings of self-doubt, disgust with one's racial group can lead to the erosion of blacks as an entire race!

What is so fascinating about **black-on-black crime** is that blacks continue to survive and persevere in spite of the chronic economic and social problems that have been perpetuating for centuries! One could easily believe that blacks are a resilient people, meaning that they are able to adapt well in the face of adversity, trauma, calamities, tragedy, and threats, with the serious health problems and financial stressors that so many encounter every day in their lives.

Chapter 4

Dynamics of Black-On-Black Crime

The dynamics of **black-on-black crime** is a complex, complicated phenomenon — a phenomenon that cannot be explained but does offer some insight. **Black-on-black crime** is not black and white. It is not about black people, exclusively. It affects <u>all</u> Americans who live in America. Furthermore, black people are not monolithic. They are different within the black race. The black race is just as diverse as other minority groups in America. For instance, when black people date each other, this process can create some interesting situations. Some blacks have their own preferences for dating. For example, some black women and men will only date a certain person whose facial features and complexion meet their expectations, as well as height, build and hair texture. Some black people only date white people, because of various reasons. Of course, this is prejudice: prejudging without the facts. Unfortunately, this does have an impact on **black-on-black crime** because it may create interracial bias, classism, fighting among themselves in an effort to "fit in." Moreover, this type of mentality causes some blacks to internalize their problematic worldviews, beliefs and values, while putting down their own people without knowing it!

Even when some blacks make it out of the *hood,* they are often criticized and accused of trying to be "white" or called "Uncle Tom" or an "Oreo," meaning being black on the outside, but trying to be white in the inside. This separates blacks more from each other, creating a class within the black race.

Reflection

Chapter 5

A Perspective of Black History

What's all the noise and fuss about black history? Why there is a resistance to teaching and learning about black history in America? Why are there some governors, politicians, policymakers, school districts, colleges, universities, Americans, etc., who refused to support teaching black history to their students, especially white students? Education is a virtue. Schools, universities and colleges taught history and historic events that took place in America for decades. Muzzles have been placed on these learning institutions. But why? I once heard one of the governors stating that Americans do not need to know how horrible they had been toward each other, meaning that white Americans do not need to be reminded of the heinous crimes and massacres that black Americans encountered at the hands of their fellow white Americans.

Black history has been in the shadows of American history for centuries because it embarrasses and shames America to the world.

Specifically, when the world learned about America's legalized racism system, e.g., the "Jim Crow" law, negative attention came upon America, shaming and ridiculing white Americans for the obdurate ways of treating African Americans, especially during slavery.

Slavery was a legalized system that existed in America for approximately 400 years at the expense of blacks who were taken from their native land, Africa.

Slavery was an abhorrent method, used to control, exploit, intimidate and kill at will blacks who were slaves. My paternal grandfather was born on a plantation and was beaten when he was a boy living on the plantation. My grandfather lived to be over 100 years old.

Slavery was a way for some states to make their living. For instance, the state of Mississippi was one of the richest states of America because of slavery. Now, it is the poorest state in America.

I have spoken to several white Americans about black history being taught in schools, and they believe black history would not benefit white children, because it would make them feel badly about how white Americans inhumanely treated black Americans. They also believe that black history should not be taught in grade schools or high schools, because white children and young teenagers would not know how to properly process the atrocities, lynching and massacres that black people, including black children, endured for centuries. Moreover, they argued that only "qualified teachers" should teach black history. The majority of the whites I've spoken about black history suspect that it is a way to divide whites and blacks, meaning there is a movement to instigate polarization, strife and division between black and white Americans.

Personally, I am a bit puzzled by all of this. It is my understanding that black Americans want their stories included in American history. Period. I don't know about this other issue about a movement precipitating polarization in America. I do realize that black history is not one of the proudest moments of American history, and it is certainly not to be forgotten or buried, as if it never happened.

Perhaps black history should not be associated with the Critical Race Theory (CRT), since there is such a negative association involving CRT. Nevertheless, black history does deserve a place in American history.

Although CRT is over 20 years old, there is a lot of controversy about it. In fact, it has been banned from some schools and some universities because of the misinformation and disinformation. Basically, CRT is a concept examined by social and civil-rights scholars and activists of how laws, social and political movements, and the media impacted social conceptions of race and ethnicity.

There is so much that America does not know about black history. For instance, the Black Wall Street massacre, the Tuskegee Experiment, the Henrietta Lacks' story, the Rosewood, Florida, massacre and the real story behind the "Great Chicago Fire" are just a few black historic events that are not written and/or fully documented in American history books.

When I shared the story about the *Black Wall Street* with some white Americans, they are appalled and shocked. They believe this type of black history should be shared with the mainstream. Many millennials never heard of the Tuskegee experience or Henrietta Lacks' story. Moreover, the vast majority of Americans, including blacks, do not know the true story about the "Great Chicago Fire."

Unfortunately, there is immense negative American history. Because of this, some believe that it should not be told, learned, or taught in the schools in America. I disagree. Black history is no different than American history, i.e., history that has blemished the "the land of the free." As I stated, history is good for history, but not for the human race.

Chapter 6

Is Black-On-Black Crime a Social Disease or a Maladaptive Behavior?

Black-on-black crime is a serious problem in America, and it has been for quite some time. I strongly believe that **black-on-black crime** is a *social disease*: a disease that is incurable but is treatable. Many people believe that this issue can only be resolved by blacks themselves. I disagree. If it were the case, I would not be writing about it. This phenomenon has impacted the black communities, to the extent that no one really knows what to do about it. Not much progress has been made to address this chronic problem in America. Even blacks do not have an answer to **black-on-**

black crime. What is so interesting about **black-on-black crime** is that it also affects <u>all</u> Americans.

As I mentioned in my previous book, there are different types of diseases and hundreds of social diseases, and **black-on-black crime** is one of them. It can also be considered as a maladaptive behavior. Maladaptive behavior can be a behavior that is abnormal in nature and psychopathological as a mental disorder or mental illness.

When I was attending graduate school, studying for my doctorate in clinical psychology, I learned that a significant number of American families are dysfunctional. One of my professors claimed that over 85% of American families are dysfunctional. A dysfunctional family tends to have constant chaos and confusion in its family dynamics. Family members are not able to come to an agreement on simple things such as meal preparation, family budget, family vacation plans, etc. Discord, dissention, despair and confrontation and domestic violence are the hallmark of dysfunctional families. Moreover, some dysfunctional families have generational cycles in their households, i.e., family history repeats itself with dysfunction from generation to generation.

The etiology of dysfunction in American families is complicated and complex, as well as idiopathic. Obviously, each family dynamics differs from family to family, as well as from generations to generations.

A social disease is no difference from a medical disease or a mental disease. What they all have in common is that diseases are incurable but are treatable. **Black-on-black crime** is treatable. I believe **black-on-black crime** can be treated with the right *antidote*. This *antidote* must include a comprehensive treatment plan, which should include economic opportunities, quality education, community involvement from black people and collaboration with public officials.

Maladaptive behavior is abnormal behavior. For instance, we know that it is not normal for families to live in constant chaos and confusion. We know that it is not normal for families to hurt and injure each other; we know that it is not normal for families to live in poverty and despair; and we know that it is not normal for families to hate each other for various reasons.

In some respect, racism has a lot to do with **black-on-black crime**, but it is not the only reason.

Some blacks are perpetuating the oppression mentality maintained by the mainstream and the stigmatization of blacks being dangerous, aimless and lazy. One of the reasons for this is the perception of blacks.

Reflection

Chapter 7

Black Hip-hop/Rap Music: As It Relates to Black-On-Black Crime

Music is just like comedy: Everyone has a preference, and there are different categories of music. For example, R&B, jazz, contemporary jazz, blues, house music, rock, hard rock, classical and Hip-hop/Rap are among the choices from which people can choose. Music is used in every aspect of our lives. We listen to music at weddings and funerals, in church, concerts, etc. Some people listen to music to help them to relax or work out. College and high school students often listen to music when they are studying. Music has a way of affecting our emotions and feelings.

During the '70s, the hip-hop/rap genre was born. This type of music was a way for blacks to express themselves, using music lyrics, rhythm, dancing and shaking their bodies. Boomboxes were blasting with this music mostly in the black communities and black youths were crazy about the sound of hip-hop/rap music. Some blacks felt it was a way to express racial oppression, injustice, *White Supremacy*, police brutality and political views. Even today hip-hop/rap is still popular. Some of the "music artists" were able to market their musical skills and made millions of dollars. Even now, some artists have made a name for themselves, as well as becoming actors, entrepreneurs and businesswomen and businessmen and wealthy!!

Interestingly, street gangs began to re-write hip-hop and rap music for different purposes. For example, some of the lyrics used were derogatory toward black females. Quite often the "N" word was used, as well as violent and malevolent words, instigating, inciting and insinuating, to the point of causing **black-on-black** crime between black gangs.

Even today hip-hop/rap music has been implicated in some of the street gang shootings and killings. As mentioned earlier, a significant number of black gang members are shot and/or killed by other black gang members. Countless drive-by shootings have taken the lives of innocent people, including children and babies. There have been reports of black families being in the wrong place at the wrong time, becoming victims of **black-on-black crime**. In many of these incidents the perpetrator(s) are never apprehended. So, the **black-on-black crime** saga continues and goes unresolved!

Surprisingly, some white people like hip-hop/rap music. Some believe it is good dancing music. But I am not sure if they are referring to the same hip-hop/rap music using derogatory and repulsive lyrics about African Americans, especially African American women.

As of late, rappers are using lyrics to express suicide, depression, and other mental health issues. I not sure what caused the change, but I suspect it is because of the tumultuous times we are living in now. There is a lot of darkness in the world. People need healing and redemption. Even the artists of hip-hop/rap music are not immune to what is happening in our society, as well as in their own personal lives. In fact, some of the hip-hop/rappers have a history of mental illness. Perhaps we will begin to see more changes in rappers' music. Hopefully, this will have a positive impact on their followers' behavior, disposition and attitude toward people.

I might be a bit biased against hip/hop/rap music. Personally, I prefer *old school music* — music that expresses love, peace, and harmony. I find *old school music* poetic, relaxing and easier to understand compared to hip-hop/rap music. I don't recall old school music using slanderous or demeaning words in its lyrics. Of course, it is a matter of one's taste and preference.

Chapter 8
No Snitching

I cannot believe there is an unwritten policy about no snitching in the *hood*, meaning that black people do not cooperate with the police and/or law enforcement during criminal investigations. Because of this problem, a lot of crimes go unresolved, and criminals get away with "murder." Personally, I cannot fathom the thought of allowing a criminal who has harmed me and/or my loved ones to get off scot-free! I believe this is a serious problem with **black-on-black crime**. How can you eradicate crime when the police do not receive any cooperation when investigating or pursing crimes committed in the black communities? How can you receive justice if law enforcement perceives you to be aloof and uncaring about solving crime in your own neighborhood? Black people need to take an active role in helping to eradicate crime in their neighborhoods. Law enforcement can only be effective if there is a collaboration and relationship between them and the people whom they serve and protect. That relationship needs to be active and proactive! Black people cannot take a passive-aggressive stand and expect crime will be resolved in their neighborhoods if they are not actively involved solving **black-on-black crime**.

I cannot believe gang members have this unwritten policy, too. A few months ago, there was news coverage about a gang member who was shot several times and was dying on the operation table. When the police were questioning the gang member about who shot him, and he knew who his shooter was, he told the police, "I ain't no snitch." Shortly after telling the police this, the young man died on the operation table.

As I was watching this news coverage, I was wondering what the deceased gang member's thought of mind was, to hold on this type of mindset with such extraordinary conviction. Unbelievable! For the life of me, I cannot make any sense or form any logic from this type of thinking, and I am a clinical psychologist who used to worked with street gangs. Obviously, street gangs fall into the category of a social disease, just like racism, poverty, discrimination, prejudice and many others. It just doesn't make any sense! As a result, the perpetrator(s) literally gets away with murder.

Now, I must make a distinction between gang members who do not believe in snitching and blacks who are not gang members who feel the same. First, the no-snitching policy among gang members and criminals has been around for decades. Gang members and criminals have this unwritten policy about not snitching on each other, regardless of being enemies. The no-snitch policy is perhaps perceived as a "badge of honor" for gang members and/or criminals. Obviously, some are willing to go to their graves knowing who's the cause of their death but refuse to disclose the identity of their perpetrator(s). Just amazing! Second, blacks who are not gang members, but become victims of **black-on-black crime**, provide a totally different acrimonious situation for law enforcement as well as in the black community. These individuals are not criminals or gang members. Hence, they do not own gang members or criminals any loyalty. However, they do own it to themselves and the black community. This is the only way justice will be given to the black communities in America. Law enforcement cannot do anything without the cooperation of blacks in the communities. Blacks have an obligation, not only to the law enforcement, but also to themselves. I do understand it is a safety and security factor, but who wants to live in constant fear for the remainder of his or her life?

Fear does play a role in this paradoxical situation, creating hopelessness and helplessness in the black community. It is almost the same as the life of a gang member who does not expect to ever live a different life.

Chapter 9

Redlining: As It Relates to Black-On-Black Crime

In 1944, President Franklin D. Roosevelt signed the GI Bill into law. The purpose of the GI Bill was to help veterans who fought in the war, to have economic opportunities and take care of their families. With the GI Bill, veterans were able to receive stipends to cover college tuition and expenses for college and trade school, earn extra points for hiring consideration and receive low-interest mortgage loans to purchase a house. I would like to point out that there were African Americans who fought in the war and were entitled to the GI Bill but were denied these benefits/privileges. Not only did this caused a great deal of resentment and defeat among the black GIs, but it also intensified despair in the black communities. In addition, many of the black GI's could not get jobs or make money. As a result, they were not able to provide for their families. In some cases, they were forced to participate in illegal activities, which involved **black-on-black crime**.

President Franklin D. Roosevelt wanted to stimulate the economy by encouraging Americans to purchase homes and property. Consequently, banks developed a zone plan that they utilized to approve or disapprove loans. The zone plan consisted of green, yellow and red. Veterans who lived in the green zone were eligible for mortgage loans. Interestingly, this zone was predominantly white or an all-white community. The yellow zone was also predominantly white, but the residents were questionable for a mortgage loan. In the red zone, where blacks lived, they were not eligible for a mortgage loan. Consequently, the "redlining" concept came into play, as we know it today.

According to the Federal Housing Authority Act (FHA), which was enacted in 1934, this was illegal. Interestingly, FHA never enforced the federal law, holding banks accountable for housing discrimination. Even today, redlining still exists.

Redlining describes the discriminatory practice of zoning of areas where banks would avoid investment, based on the racial makeup of the black communities. So, the black GI's who lived in a red zone area did not qualify for a mortgage loan. Unbelievable!

To some extent, this has changed, but not on a large scale. Black GI's or black veterans can receive the GI bill. However, banks are still reluctant to give out loans where the neighborhood is predominantly black.

Usually, in the redlining areas, property value depreciates, businesses move out, services decline, poverty intensifies and **black-on-black crime** becomes rampant.

Redlining does not dissipate overnight. It is a social disease that <u>strategically</u> disappears once the "five-year plan" is implemented. Sometimes it takes years before the plan is launched. In the meantime, black communities continue to suffer and blacks slowly die at the hands of other blacks.

Reflection

Chapter 10

Black-On-Black Crime vs. White-On-White Crime

In comparison to white crime, blacks have a higher incidence of rape, robbery and aggravated assault than whites, who are likely to be victims of simple assault, as reported by the DOJ. Younger black males have a higher incidence of violence than older black males.

Black males have the highest homicide rate, followed by black females, white males and white females, respectively.

African Americans who are single and between the age of 16 and 24 have the highest victimization of burglary compared to non-African Americans. In fact, burglary is the most prevalent crime of **black-on-black crime**, followed by aggravated assault and robbery. In comparison to blacks, whites have much lower rates in the aforementioned categories. When the numbers are compared between the suburbs and inner cities, they are even lower for whites and black, respectively. However, blacks still have higher crime rates than their counterparts. This information is reported by DOJ.

Of the 94% of the black homicide cases, blacks have killed other blacks; and in 83% of the white homicide cases, white people have killed other white people. What this tells me is that blacks and whites are more than likely to commit homicide amongst themselves. Sadly, I am not surprised at the percentage of blacks killing blacks. However, I am very surprised to learn that the high percentage of white people killing each other. I would not have thought this would be the case. When I looked at the two percentages, I don't see a significant difference. This was not the case 30 or 50 years ago. It seems that America has become more violent and homicidal compared to the past years. Based on this, people are handling their differences with guns and killing each other. Both black people and white people are guilty of this! Interestingly, **black-on-black crime** receives more attention from the media than white-on-white crime. I am not sure why this is the case, but it makes a good argument with the media. I am not sure it makes a difference to address white-on-white crime relative to **black-on-black crime**. Perhaps the media may believe that **black-on-black crime** is more newsworthy. However, this gives the impression that white people don't have an issue with killing each other. Obviously, this could not be the case, as evidenced by the DOJ statistics. Quite interesting!

The victim usually knows his or her assailant. Also, victims of crime are often killed with a weapon. In many cases, this involves a handgun. Moreover, poor whites and poor blacks commit the majority of the crimes and killings in the United States of America. One would wonder whether poverty is a factor. On the surface, it seems that way. However, underlying issues are different for blacks and whites in this regard. For instance, the justice system is not the same for poor whites as for poor blacks. A poor black man and a poor white man can commit the same crime but receives different fines or punishment. In fact, the penalty would be harsher for the black man than for the white man. Interesting! So, where does poverty fit into this equation? Actually, it really does not. Poverty is based on income. So, a person who used to be poor or lived in an impoverished neighborhood does not mean he or she will become a criminal. So, what does poverty has to do with committing a crime, especially murder?

There might be a correlation between the increased homicide rate and gun laws. As you may have noticed, many of our states have passed gun laws, legalizing citizens to carry concealed handguns. We can thank our *Constitution* for this, meaning the right to bear arms.

According to DOJ, in 77% of the homicide cases, blacks were killed with guns and whites were killed 60% of the homicide cases with guns. In these cases, over 60% of the victims and offenders were males, meaning that black and white males were both the victims and perpetrators of the homicide cases. Another interesting statistic is that children under the age of 5 were killed 80% of the time by a father or another male. I found these numbers egregious and depressing!

I found something else quite interesting in reference to violent crime in America: DOJ reports that whites commit 50% of the violent crimes in America, yet they are 62% of the population. Blacks commit 25% of the violent crime in America, but they are only 12% of the population. Hispanics have 19% of the criminal cases in America, and they are 17% of the population. And Asians are charged with 1% of crime in America, but they are 6% of the population in this country. Moreover, 82% of the violent crime black males committed was against other black males. This is so amazing because this attributes to the endangered species of black men phenomenon. If this continues, black men will be extinct. When this will happen, no one knows. But it will happen if there is no turnaround. This is so sad and unfortunate!

Young youth (ages 12 to 17) and young adults (ages 18 to 29) are committing the majority of the violent crime in America. This also applies to the white population. After the age of 30, there is a decline in the offender-victim ratio for both whites and blacks.

Chapter 11
Gentrification: As It Relates to Black-On-Black Crime

Gentrification, a process that tends to displace African Americans and cause economic despair, is used in predominantly black communities, in order to develop new housing and create new businesses. Economically, gentrification seems to be positive for the business world, but not for blacks! As far as blacks are concerned, there is nothing positive about gentrification. In fact, it causes more harm than good for them. Blacks are literally forced out of their homes and neighborhoods and have nowhere else to live or go.

Gentrification does attract new affluent residents and brings an improved infrastructure to the community. In the middle of the transformation, **black-on-black crime** intensifies.

When blacks are dislocated from their original neighborhoods, they tend to relocate to areas where mostly blacks migrate. These areas often do not have affordable housing and blacks are usually not welcomed.

Because of the lack of affordable housing, many blacks become homeless. This is the aftermath of gentrification and the continuation of **black-on-black crime**.

In 1964, the Civil Rights Act was adopted and passed into law, giving blacks a chance to live decent lives. In theory, this Act prohibited unfair treatment and practices in reference to employment, hiring practices, job opportunities, school segregation, housing, etc., for blacks. Unfortunately, this Act was virtually *repealed* by the late president Ronald Reagan. This administration thwarted any possibilities for blacks to benefit from the Civil Rights Act, as it was intended to be executed into law. Even when Congress passed the Civil Rights Act, blacks were not completely benefiting from it. There was still unfair treatment and racial discrimination in America. But when Ronald Reagan became president, everything came to a complete halt! Blacks were suffering tremendously. Jobs and decent housing were scare. Schools in black neighborhoods were deplorable and dilapidated and without sufficient funds and resources. Since then, it has been an uphill battle for blacks to live in America.

Historically, blacks have been forced to deal with redlining and gentrification. And people wonder why blacks cannot help themselves or live better lives. As stated previously, other minority groups do not encounter gentrification or redlining, to the extent that blacks do. Interestingly, people, in general, are not familiar with gentrification or redlining. Both have a devastating impact on black communities, especially the impoverished, marginalized, and disenfranchised blacks.

Gentrification and redlining are concepts that are normally <u>not</u> discussed in board rooms and/or meetings where business deals are made between banks and corporate America. Gentrification is an unspoken policy that has been in existence since post World War II.

Reflection

Chapter 12
A Comparative Analysis of Domestic Violence Between Black and White Families

Domestic violence is a serious problem in America. I don't believe any race is immune to it. However, domestic violence is treated and viewed differently between white families and black families. For instance, based on the research I reviewed, white domestic violence is not covered in the same fashion by the media in comparison to black domestic violence in America. Even though there is a 11% margin difference between the two races, black violence tends to receive more negative attention from the media, giving the impression that black families have more violence in their families. When looking at the numbers from DOJ, i.e., 94% of **black-on-black crime** involves the perpetrators and victims being black; and 83% of white-on-white crime involves the perpetrators and victims being white demonstrates that crime is rampant in America. However, if this is the case, why the disparaging of the news coverage, meaning white crime is not considered as newsworthy as black crime? Interesting!

With black families and white families, domestic violence usually involves death; the wife is usually killed by her husband. Hence, domestic violence becomes fatal. What is more interesting is that the number of domestic violence cases go unreported. Traditionally, the victim would not report the incident and/or press charges against the perpetrator. In many cases, the perpetrator is the husband. Now there are laws that protect the victim even if she or he does not call the police or file a complaint. Sometimes neighbors report domestic violence. When the police come to the residence and there is evidence of injuries or bruises, the perpetrator can be arrested even without a complaint filed by the spouse.

Interestingly, the domestic violence cases are handled differently, meaning that white perpetrators are usually prosecuted with a lessen punishment compared to black perpetrators. The reason(s) is not clear. Unfortunately, the DOJ does not provide any statistical analyses to explain/offer the reason(s) why white and black perpetrators are indicted and prosecuted in a different fashion. One can only speculate that race is a factor, as well as SES.

Chapter 13
The White Flight: As It Relates to Black-On-Black Crime

As America has become more diverse, people tend to misbehave. Furthermore, it seems that the more diverse we are, the more divided America has become. For instance, when a community has been predominantly one race for years and years and other people move into the community, racism rears its ugly head. In some cases, there is the *white flight.* The *white flight* is a term that is often used, to describe whites leaving their communities when blacks move in. When white people move out of the neighborhood, property value depreciates, businesses move out, redlining starts, poverty occurs, services decline, and **black-on-black** crime increases.

The white flight does have an impact on **black-on-black crime** in ways you wouldn't imagine. For instance, a community that was once flourishing has now become a hellhole for blacks. Blacks are left with meager resources that do not sustain them. Typically, when whites move, their property is in poor condition, needing repairs and maintenance. Something that most blacks are not able to afford when they first move into their new homes.

The correlation between *redlining* and *white flight* is quite intriguing and remarkable, meaning that blacks are not able to secure resources in order to sustain and maintain their style of living. Banks refused to lend money to blacks who live in *white flight* neighborhoods due to *redlining.*

Consequently, blacks are left to fend for themselves. Sometimes this may mean to attack, steal, from and kill each other. This sounds so horrible, and it is. It is just a fact of life for many blacks who have been victims of the *white flight*.

Reflection

Chapter 14
Carjacking

Carjacking has become an illegal money-making industry. White people are now affected by it, too. It is totally out of control and has become a crisis in inner cities and urban areas in America! Young black youth, as young as 12 years old, are forcing people out of their cars at gunpoint and stealing them. In some incidents, the victims are killed in the process of their cars being stolen.

During the month of July 2022, in the Ukraine Village of Chicago, a white father and his son were forced out of their SUV. This carjacking occurred in broad daylight! When the father was interviewed, he acknowledged Chicago always had its problems, but "Not like this," he claimed. The truth of the matter is that Chicago has always been a dangerous city to live in. When carjacking occurs in the black communities in Chicago, no one seems to be concerned. But, now since carjacking is spreading more and more into the white communities in Chicago, white people are becoming alarmed. Carjacking is not a black problem, but a crisis in America. It would be interesting to see if changes will occur to combat this nation-wide crisis, since white people are impacted, too.

Carjacking initially started in the *hood*. Now there have been reports of it occurring outside the black communities. As I have stated numerous times, racism affects <u>everyone</u>, including non-African Americans.

Auto theft is a serious problem in America, but it is more of a serious problem in the black communities, which is why auto insurance is significantly more for the average black person living in a black community. In some cases, some blacks are not able to get affordable auto insurance due to the high risk of auto theft.

Auto thieves make their living stealing cars. Of course, I am not insinuating only auto thieves are black. Since I am talking about **black-on-black crime**, I believe it is appropriate to mention this type of crime in this book, as it relates to black people. Blacks are randomly victims of carjacking.

Perhaps it is because the make and model of their cars and the location where they are driving. Carjacking occurs anywhere and everywhere and at any time, including in broad daylight.

Chapter 15

A Perspective of People of Color

Interestingly, the term "people of color" has become the latest phrase the media are utilizing to identify minorities, placing them in one category, as well as the acronym *BIPOC* or Black, Indigenous, and People of Color. I have a problem with both, because it gives the impression that all minorities are monolithic, which is so far from the truth. This topic would require another book to write, so I am not going to discuss details. However, this topic does deserve some discussion in this book, as it relates to **black-on-black crime**.

For years, the federal government has used different categories to place Americans in order to keep count of the population and to maintain demographics and compositions. These categories have changed remarkably over the years. For instance, blacks/African Americans were once identified as "Colored." This term was used mostly during the *Jim Crow* era. Then the categories changed numerous times from Negro, Afro American, Black, and now African American. The terms black and African American are still used interchangeably by some non-African Americans, including the media. I believe most African Americans prefer to be identified as African Americans or American. I guess now the latter is becoming a new race category for some people. What's my point?

In order for African American, aka blacks, to receive full recognition for their needs, as a race, we should not be placed in a category for all minorities. In fact, I would say the same for all minority/ethnic groups. It serves no purpose to bunch all minorities in a category such as "People of Color" or BIPOC or minorities. I am not sure why the federal government and media <u>continue</u> do this.

African Americans are different from other minority/ethnic groups, and other minority/ethnic groups are different from African Americans and each other. When I hear the term "people of color" describing African Americans or blacks, I believe this creates confusion and lacks respect for all minorities. For instance, it is misleading and disrespectful to place Italian Americans, Greek American with Irish Americans as the white race. All have different customs, foods, music, lifestyle, beliefs, etc. The same can be said about Chinese Americans, Japanese Americans, Korean Americans, Indian Americans, and South Pacific groups, yet they are considered to be the Asian race. Mexican Americans and Puerto Rican Americans and other Spanish speaking races are placed in the Hispanic category. Again, each ethnic group is distinctively different with its own idiosyncrasies. What is my point? When the federal government and the media use only minority, Hispanic or white, I believe this devalues the entire human race, ignoring each race and ethnic group as different with different needs. For example, the needs for

African Americans are different from other ethnic groups. African Americans tends to have more dire needs compared to other race and ethnic groups. Placing all "minorities" in the same category minimizes their unique challenges.

Reflection

Chapter 16
The Majority Becomes the Minority and the Minority Becomes the Majority

Prior to World War II, the population of the United State of America was over 85% white. Now, the number has shrunk to approximately 63%. The Hispanic population is approximately 18%. Blacks compose of approximately 13% of the American population. The Asian population is approximately 6%. It is my belief that there is an unreasonable fear about the changes of the composition in America. Some people believe that minorities are taking over the country. When Barack Obama was elected as president, gun sales reached an all-time high. There were more attacks on blacks, especially black men. **Black-on-black crime** across the nation was rampant. There was so much fear in the country and still is the case. What is so interesting about all of this is that blacks are getting it from both ends: Blacks are killing blacks and whites are killing blacks. As I mentioned previously, blacks have been in America over the past 500 years, yet the black population has not increased that much due to the high adult mortality and infant mortality rates. Interestingly, white people are not being killed by blacks more. However, there are more white people killing each other. But the white infant mortality rate is not an issue. White women are not having babies as they used to prior to World War II. Fewer white babies are born every year in America, which has impacted the white population for decades! Consequently, white people are slowly becoming the minority. It is projected that by the year 2050 whites will become the minority group and the current minority groups will become the majority in United States of America. I believe this is causing a lot of *pseudo fear* in our country.

Reflection

Chapter 17

A Perspective of Black Mortality

Blacks have the highest infant mortality and adult mortality rates, yet they are only 13% of the population in America! Amazing!! As stated previously, blacks are overrepresented in all categories of crimes, especially the homicide category. Black males between the ages of 18 to 24 experienced the highest homicide and criminal activity rates. In other words, black men are dying and killing each other at an alarming rate, 77% and 90%, respectively. This is difficult for me to believe. I had an idea that the numbers were high, but not this high. This is so unbelievable!!

Because of the chronic high infant mortality and adult mortality rates, the population of the African American race has not grown. This seems interesting, because blacks have been living in America over 500 years, yet the population rate remains <u>constant</u>. Since I have been studying the demographics of African Americans, which has been over 30 years, I don't recall if the population rate has ever been over 13%. For the longest it has always been approximately 12% or 12.5%. This is so amazing.

Black-on-black crime is the culprit in the black communities in America. When I used to work with gang members, many of them told me that they did not expect to live past the age of 18.

According to DOJ, 24% of gang members were victims of homicide under the age of 18, and juveniles were also 19% of the victims of homicide. Well, this self-fulling prophecy has come to past for many of them. **Black-on-black crime** is a hard life to live and a very short one, too.

Reflection

Chapter 18

The American Dream: As It Relates to Black-On-Black Crime

Activist Stokely Carmichael once stated that if hard work paid off, Jews and blacks would be the richest people in the world. For years I have been told to work hard, and you will be successful. Now, I am not too sure about this. I don't believe black people have a problem working hard, but their hard work does not always pay off.

The American Dream implies that anyone who works hard will reap the benefits of his or her labor, making it to the societal hierarchy. Obviously, this does not apply to blacks. Black people continue to work hard but are not reaping from their efforts. What is so amazing about this is that blacks are criticized for their plight. Many non-Americans believe that some blacks do not work hard enough, in order to make their lives better. This is totally absurd!

I have been living in America over 67 years and still don't know what the *American Dream* really means. I believe I am a hard worker, industrious, ambition, driven and determined, yet I do not believe I am where I am supposed to be in the world if I am to believe in the *American Dream* concept. I actually live a modest lifestyle.

Economic opportunities need to be at the helm of success for black people so that they will be able to attain and achieve the *American Dream*.

Without economic resources and a solid infrastructure, it is likely that the majority of black people will continue to suffer economically, spiritually, and morally in their black communities, as well as in society.

In order to eradicate **black-on-black crime** in the black communities, you need to replace it with economic success! Interestingly, **black-on-black crime** generates a lot of revenue for the black communities. For example, we all know drug trafficking is a lucrative *commodity* in the *hood*, but many lives are lost, and families are destroyed. What's more interesting is that the money does not stay in the black communities. Where does the money go? Can you imagine if all the drug money stayed in the black communities? Poverty or unemployment would not exist. Black people would have a way to survive and make a living. Of course, I am not advocating drug trafficking or any other illegal activity. I am just pondering the thought of the money from drug trafficking that would significantly benefit the black communities in America. Obviously, some people are benefiting from drug trafficking, but I don't believe this includes the black people who live in the black communities.

Economics determines where people live, how they live, and what they can afford. In the inner-city communities and some urban areas in America, where a significant number of blacks live, the economy is normally depressed. Usually, blacks have the highest unemployment rate and are jobless more often than white people; blacks pay more for food, gas, auto insurance compared to whites in their communities. Services in black communities, such as public schools, garbage collection, street repairs and fire and police safety and protection, are inferior to other communities. Poverty is rampant in these communities as well as **black-on-black crime**.

America is not just polarized as a country, but the individual races are polarized among themselves. What do I mean by this? Among the ethnic groups, there is hatred, prejudice and jealousy, to the extent that Americans are antagonistic and acrimonious toward their fellow Americans, which is one of the main reasons our society is so violent and vicious. This obstructs camaraderie, trust, respect and solidarity in our country. **Black-on-black crime** is a product of this polarization, as well as self-hatred.

Chapter 19
L.I.T.S. (Leadership Integrating Tomorrow's Souls)

Now, what can we do about **black-on-black crime** in America? Shortly after writing my first book, I had a vision of how this social disease can be eradicated. As I mentioned earlier, I am a pragmatic, visionary person. Consequently, I created **L.I.T.S.**, aka, *Leadership Integrating Tomorrow's Souls*. I envisioned this concept to become a reality in the black communities, enabling leadership to lead the way to combat and eradicate **black-on-black crime** in America. What do I mean by this? First, leadership needs to be established in the black communities. Right now, there is no leadership. Leadership begins with oneself, meaning that all Americans are called to the cause. This is not a black people problem; it's America's problem. Therefore, the approach is to involve <u>all</u> Americans! Second, with the proper leadership, guidance, and direction, African American youth can have a sense of direction and purpose in life; and with the proper leadership, African American families can receive support and resources. As I mentioned in my previous book, the black communities are not able to combat **black-on-black crime** independently.

Third, I would like to see quality education invested in the black communities. Quality education creates economic opportunities. Even though compulsory education is mandated, it does not mean that students will be prepared to compete in the market world. Without a quality education, a black child doesn't have a chance in this world. Employers often claim that they cannot find qualified blacks to hire. There may be some validity to this, but there are cases that qualified, skilled blacks do not get hired for various reasons.

Also, I would like to see universal health care in black communities. Having universal health care would enable African Americans to receive the proper health care they deserve. During the pandemic, there were so many African Americans without proper health care. People need quality health care, and universal health care can make this happen.

Having universal education and universal health care in the black communities may resolve most of the problems perpetuated by **black-on-black crime**. Both would significantly enhance the quality of life for blacks who live in impoverished neighborhoods and have disenfranchised and impoverished lives!

Finally, it is my belief that when people are educated and provided with quality health care, they are likely to become respectful and industrialized citizens, as well as unlikely to get involved in **black-on-black crime**. Of course, there are exceptions! People who are not educated and not provided with quality health care are likely to become frustrated, angry, and aggressive toward each other. Right now, we see the impact **black-on-black crime** has taken a toll on inner city black communities in America. For instance, Chicago, where I was reared, lived and worked for many years, has one of the highest homicide rates in America, mainly due to **black-on-black crime**. In fact, in the years of 2000 and 2001, it ranked number one in the country having the highest homicide rate back-to-back years. A significant number of murder rates involved **black-on-black crime**, blacks killing and murdering each other. Unbelievable and shameful!

Having economic opportunities in black communities would make a colossal difference in African Americans' lives. For example, small business loans provided to striving African Americans would give them the opportunity to bring businesses to the black communities, as well as stimulating the economy in the black neighborhoods. African Americans who are savvy in business can help train other blacks to become business owners, starting with pre-teens and teenagers who may want to attend college and learn how to become business owners themselves.

I cannot over emphasize the importance of economic opportunity for the black communities. Hence, money makes a world of difference in people's lives. Without it, people cannot survive. People need to make a living for themselves and their families. This is what life is all about! I am so amazed that the mainstream has not realized this or just doesn't care. If black people are expected to *pull themselves by their bootstraps*, they need the economic tools to do this.

I have heard the argument that people from Cambodia, Vietnam, and the Philippines, just to mention a few, are able to come to America and strive and become successful. What people fail to realize and/or refuse to admit is that these individuals do not have the level of racism African Americans have in their communities. I am talking about *redlining* and *gentrification*, for examples.

Redlining and *gentrification* have been major barriers in the black communities for decades. *Redlining* and *gentrification* only exist in black communities, not in other minority communities. Once these elements are removed from the black communities, you will see a major difference. I guarantee you this!!

In essence, getting all Americans involved is perhaps the only way to eradicate **black-on-black crime.** I don't believe leaving the problem up to blacks to fix will ever happen. Black people do not have the resources or power to resolve **black-on-black crime** in their communities.

One may think blacks should be able to fix their own problem. This is far from the truth. Just because **black-on-black crime** is predominantly in black communities does not mean that black people are the reasons that this problem exists, chronically. I know this for a fact, because my family and I have lived in black communities, and we were not the cause of the problem.

Black-on-black crime is often portrayed by the media as a black people problem. The media seldom show anything positive about the black community combating **black-on-black crime.** Perhaps the media believe that **black-on-black crime** is a hopeless situation in the black community. I would like to see the media become supportive of the black causes in the black communities in America, by advocating and reporting positive news coverage about black people in America, especially black men.

On a final note, I propose that schools, colleges, and universities, starting from middle school, collaborate with black parents and youth, to raise awareness of racism impacting interracial relations and relationships among blacks in their black communities regarding **black-on-black crime** in America. As stated earlier, some blacks have been historically influenced by the mentality of being black is bad in America. As a result, they, themselves, have inherited the negative thoughts, stigmatization of black people, especially black males, are violent, dangerous, illiterate and shiftless, and lazy. This type of thinking needs to be transformed, and blacks who think and feel this way need to be re-conditioned. What do I mean by this? First, blacks are not monolithic, meaning they are not all the same. However, the mainstream, as well as the media, tend to put all blacks in a category, labeling them and perceiving them in the same way. In some cases, some blacks are guilty of this, too.

Black people need to learn how to respect themselves and each other. Respect does not exist in the black community. Black children do not respect black adults, and black children and adults do not respect black elders. Moreover, black children do not know what it means to respect adults.

One of the reasons for the lack of respect in the black community is because there is no respect for life! Teaching blacks about respecting life will enable them to respect themselves and each other.

Life is about relationships. Healthy relationships enable people to get along with their brethren. When relationships are healthy, people are healthy. People tend to help each other when they need help.

I believe children need three basic things in life: unconditional love, care, and discipline (teaching and training). Children need to know that they are loved unconditionally. When a child knows that he or she is loved unconditionally, he or she will do anything and everything for you. It is the nature of a child wanting to please and trust. However, once that trust has been violated, the child will become problematic and develop maladaptive behavior. Maladaptive behavior can be one of the precursors of criminal behavior, including **black-on-black crime**.

Providing children with care is essential and vital. Children need proper care such as food, clothes, and shelter. Parents are obligated to make sure that their children are given proper sustenance so that their children will be able to have the opportunity to live healthy and productive lives.

Oftentimes, when people hear the word *discipline*, they think of punitive punishment such as spanking and/or beating. I am not talking about this. I am talking about teaching children about values, morals, manners, respect, etc., so that they will be trained to care for themselves properly and respectfully, as well as live productive and healthy lives.

www.ingramcontent.com/pod-product-compliance
Lightning Source LLC
Chambersburg PA
CBHW071216160426
43196CB00012B/2322